CELLS

WRITTEN BY
JOHN WOOD

BookLife
PUBLISHING

©2019
Book Life
King's Lynn
Norfolk PE30 4LS

ISBN: 978-1-78637-463-9

Written by:
John Wood

Edited by:
Holly Duhig

Designed by:
Amy Li

CONTENTS

Words that look like **this** can be found in the glossary on page 31.

There is a machine that can solve difficult problems. It can learn complicated things. This machine can move around and jump up high. If the machine gets a **virus**, it can often cure itself – and if the machine gets broken, it can often fix itself. It is made up of **billions** and billions of parts, and it even grows bigger.

THIS MACHINE... IS THE HUMAN BODY.

YOUR BODY IS ALWAYS LOOKING OUT FOR YOU AND HELPING YOU OUT.

YOUR BRILLIANT BODY

Every day, your body does incredible things to keep you alive. You are probably not even aware of what it is doing most of the time. However, under your skin, all the parts of your body are working together to keep you healthy and ready for the day ahead. Do you ever think about what happens to your food after it disappears down your throat? Or why your body becomes so snotty, sweaty and sick-y when you are ill? What about how you can breathe without thinking? Your body does a lot of things **automatically**.

EVERY BODY NEEDS A BRAIN

THE HUMAN BRAIN

Your brain, sitting in your head right now, is the most amazing part. Human brains are so complicated, we still don't really understand everything about them. There are around 100 billion nerve cells in the brain – these are the things that carry messages around the brain and body. But the brain would be pretty useless on its own. What makes your body amazing is how it all fits together. It's time to go under your skin and find out how it all works.

THE DOCTOR IS HERE

Hi! My name is Seymour Skinless, and I am the world's smallest doctor – the only doctor small enough to go under the skin and find out exactly what is wrong! You must be my assistant. Well, you are just in time – we have a patient here who is very ill. I think there is something wrong with his cells. You know what a cell is, right? Well, don't worry, soon you will – we are about to go inside his body and find out all about it.

Right, let's shrink you down to my size and go inside...

WHAT SEEMS TO BE THE
PROBLEM?

WHAT IS A CELL?

Cells are the building blocks that make up all living things. There are lots of different types of cell, and each type has a different job to do. Almost all cells are much too small to be seen with your eyes. Many human cells are around 20 micrometres across – this is so small that it would take 10,000 of them to cover the head of a pin. To see them, you would need something called a microscope. This is an **instrument** that makes small things look bigger. Scientists can see cells if they look at them through a microscope.

MICROSCOPE

CELLS UNDER A MICROSCOPE

HOW MANY CELLS ARE THERE

IN YOUR BODY?

Just like a beach is made of lots of grains of sand, you are made of lots of little cells. Luckily your cells are joined together tightly, and work with each other to help you do things such as breathing, eating and moving. Some living things are made up of just one cell, while others are made of lots more. Your body is made up of trillions of cells.

THERE ARE AROUND 200 DIFFERENT TYPES OF CELLS IN THE HUMAN BODY.

WHAT DO CELLS NEED?

Cells need all sorts of things to work properly. One of the most important things for cells is a **gas** called oxygen (say: ox-ee-jen), which we get from the air we breathe. They also need energy, which we get from the food we eat. Without these things, cells would stop working and eventually die. This would be a big problem for us. For example, if the cells in our heart stopped working, then the heart wouldn't pump blood around the body. This would be very bad indeed.

The heart, which is in your chest, is one of the most important **organs** in your body.

THE HEART

HAPPY CELLS

It is important to stay healthy so that your cells are healthy too. Eating a **balanced diet** full of lots of fruit and vegetables will give your cells all the energy they need. Exercise is also a good way to look after your body, and make your cells stronger.

SPORTS ARE A GOOD WAY TO EXERCISE.

Trillions of cells! It's going to take forever to check them all! Well, my brainy assistant, we better get stuck in. You go to page 8 and start looking there, I'll start here. Hmm, this one looks fine... so does this one ... oh dear, this one's on fire...

FIRST, GO TO THE
FINGERS

If you look down at your fingers, it might seem hard to believe that they are made of tiny cells. But what are cells made of? It is time to zoom in even further and go to a place that even seems small to me – the inside of a cell!

PARTS OF A CELL

Different living things have different cells. For example, **bacteria** cells are very different from plant cells. Animal cells are very complicated and have lots of parts inside. Some of these parts are called organelles. Organelles have different jobs, but they work together to keep the cell healthy. Each organelle has its own **membrane**, which keeps it separate from the other parts of the cell.

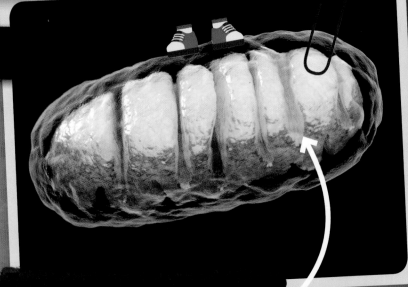

THIS IS AN ORGANELLE WITH A MEMBRANE PROTECTING IT.

CELL SHAPES

CELL SHAPE

Cells can have lots of different shapes. Plant cells are normally more square-shaped than animal cells. Bacteria cells are often round or sausage-shaped. However, even animal cells can look very different from each other. Some human cells are long and thin, like brain cells. Others, like some blood cells, are often round.

YOUR SKIN CELLS ARE QUITE FLAT AND HAVE AROUND 14 SIDES!

INSIDE A CELL

HERE ARE SOME OF THE MOST IMPORTANT PARTS OF
A CELL. LET'S TAKE A LOOK AT A SIMPLE, ROUND CELL.

CYTOPLASM is the jelly-like filling of a cell, which everything else sits in. It is see-through and mostly made of water.

The **CELL MEMBRANE** is the outer wall of the cell. It stops all the other parts of the cell floating away. The cell membrane can let certain things in and out of the cell.

MITOCHONDRIA turns food into energy.

CENTRIOLES are organelles which help the cell split in two. We will learn about cell splitting on page 12–13.

The **NUCLEUS** is like the brain of the cell. It contains information that tells the cell what to do.

LYSOSOMES (say: lie-suh-sowms) and **PEROXISOMES** (say: per-ox-ee-sowms) are like the recycling bins of the cell. Waste and rubbish are destroyed here, or turned into something new that the cell can use. These organelles also deal with anything dangerous that comes into the cell.

VACUOLES are very small, empty spaces in the cell which are used to store spare food or waste.

Here in the hand, there are lots of special cells working together, like **muscle** cells, skin cells and bone cells. We all have these same types of cells inside of us. However, if we are all made of the same cells, then why are we all so different? It is all to do with something called DNA.

WHAT IS DNA?

Your DNA is a set of information all about you. It is kept in the nucleus of your cells. Almost every cell in your body contains a copy of your DNA. Cells use DNA as a list of instructions – it tells them all sorts of things such as what colour your eyes should be, or if your hair should be curly or straight. Your DNA is a mix of your parents' DNA. This means that the set of instructions to make you is similar to the set of instructions to make your family.

FAMILIES USUALLY LOOK A LOT LIKE EACH OTHER BECAUSE THEIR DNA IS SIMILAR.

CELL NUCLEUS

Your DNA is made up of long chains of **chemicals**. The chemicals connect together in different patterns and these patterns create a secret code. This is the code that tells the cells how to make you. When these long chains of DNA are put together, they are called genes.

DNA FITS TOGETHER IN A TWISTED LADDER SHAPE.

HUMANS HAVE AROUND 20,000 – 25,000 GENES.

99% of our DNA is the same as every other human being. However, the last 1% isn't, and this is what makes everyone a little different from each other. Although your genes are probably very similar to your parents', they won't be exactly the same. Every single person has their own special set of genes.

OUR GENES AREN'T EXACTLY THE SAME. THIS MEANS WE ALL HAVE OUR OWN FINGERPRINT.

There's a gene for everything. Some control your height. This gene here tells your cells how many noses you should have. Maybe one day in the future, we might be able to change someone's DNA in any way we want. We could cure millions of people from terrible illnesses... or we could give children two noses if they haven't been good. That's science, kids.

BACK UP THE
ARM
BONES

Arm bones are some of the biggest bones in your body. But they weren't always very big. As you know, our bodies grow a lot from when we are babies to when we are adults. However, most cells do not grow bigger. Instead they split in two and create copies of themselves. When cells split in two it is called dividing. As a living thing grows, more cells are created.

CELLS OFTEN DIVIDE IN HALF, RIGHT DOWN THE MIDDLE.

NEARLY 2 TRILLION CELLS DIVIDE EVERY DAY.

PARENT CELL

DAUGHTER CELLS

DIVIDED WE STAND

However, as well as growth, there are many other reasons that cells divide. Cells have to divide to replace old cells that die. If we get cut or injured, new cells are also needed to repair the damage. The cell that splits in two is called the parent cell, and the two new cells which are created are called daughter cells. Before a cell divides, it creates a copy of the DNA, so each daughter cell will have one. Both new cells will be exactly the same as each other.

SKIN CELLS ON THE TOP LAYER OF OUR SKIN ARE LOST ALL THE TIME.

STEM CELLS

Bones are hard on the outside, but they have a spongey inside called bone marrow. Bone marrow contains stem cells. Stem cells are special because they are able to turn into all different types of cells. They are very important when it comes to repairing the body and helping it grow. This is because they can keep dividing over and over again. Stem cells can be found in other places as well, such as the brain, heart and liver.

BONE MARROW

Stem cells are a bit like superheroes that just haven't decided HOW they are going to save the world yet. They are pretty awesome!

ADULTS VS BABIES

Not all stem cells are the same. When a woman is **pregnant**, and the baby grows in her body, the baby starts off life as a single stem cell. Baby stem cells are special because they can turn into any cell in the human body when they divide.

However, adult stem cells are different. Adult stem cells can only grow into certain types of cells, depending on where the stem cell came from.

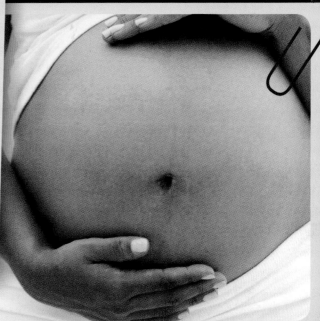

BABIES GROW IN A PART OF THEIR MOTHER'S BODY, CALLED THE WOMB.

YOUR BODY IS ALWAYS CHANGING.

Cells don't last forever. Some get too damaged or broken to work, while others get completely destroyed. Even if a cell lives a healthy life, most of them get old and break up. In every minute that goes by, your old, broken cells are being replaced by new cells. This is to stop the body getting too worn out. As your cells get replaced, so do your body parts.

HOW QUICKLY ARE CELLS REPLACED?

Different types of cells have different lifespans. For example, the cells in your colon only last a few days. They are replaced very quickly – so quickly that you have a completely new top layer of a colon every single week. However, other cells can last months or even years. This means it takes longer for other body parts to become completely new. For example, it will take a few weeks for all of the cells in your skin to be different and new.

YOUR SKELETON IS COMPLETELY REPLACED AROUND EVERY TEN YEARS OR MORE.

So what makes you... you? Are you the same person that you were when you were born? You don't have the same skin, that's for sure. If this scares you, don't worry. There is a reason I've brought you to the brain. It's time to meet the cells that have always stuck with you, through thick and thin.

BEST FRIENDS FOREVER

In some areas of the brain, there are some nerve cells that are never replaced – they last as long as you do. There are also certain cells found in your eyes that will stay with you for your whole life too.

THIS IS THE AREA OF THE BRAIN WHERE CELLS ARE NOT REPLACED.

HUMAN HEART

Heart cells aren't replaced as quickly as most cells. Usually, if there is any damage to the heart, some of the cells may be replaced with **scar tissue**. Although heart cells do replace themselves, they do this very slowly, so most of them will stick around for most of your life.

The slow **rate** at which your heart cells are replaced gets even slower as you get older.

THROUGH THE
THROAT

Look out! Pizza! It is dangerous here in the throat with all this food falling down. But what happens to the food as it goes through the body? How does it get to the cells?

BREAK IT DOWN

Our stomachs and **intestines** break down food to get all the **nutrients** out of it (see page 20–21). These parts of the body have special juices which help break down the food. Water and nutrients are absorbed by the intestines and sent round the body using the **bloodstream**. The nutrients are small enough that cells can use them to make energy. Anything that is not absorbed becomes poo.

THE TUBES AND ORGANS THAT YOU USE TO EAT FOOD AND GET RID OF POO ARE CALLED THE DIGESTIVE SYSTEM.

MITOCHONDRIA

Mitochondria (say: my-toe-con-dree-ah) are organelles in cells that are in charge of making energy. Every cell needs energy, so it can keep working to keep us alive. Without energy, the cells would die. Some cells have no mitochondria, such as red blood cells, whereas some cells have hundreds or thousands of them, such as liver cells.

MITOCHONDRIA

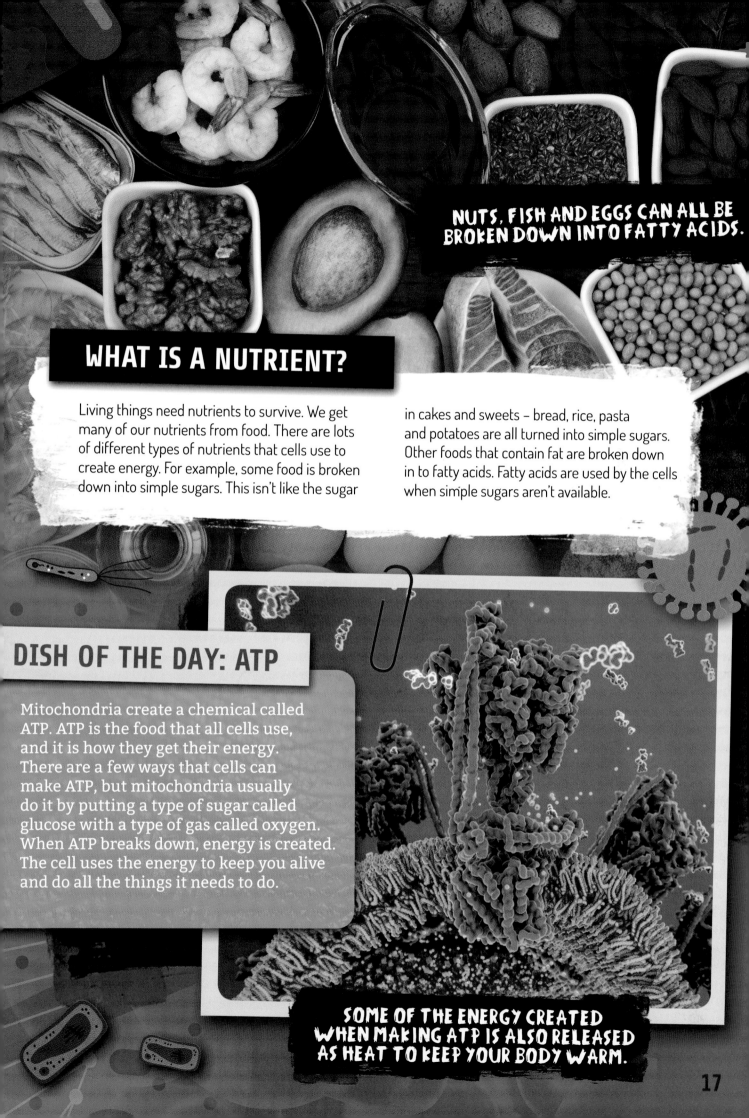

NUTS, FISH AND EGGS CAN ALL BE BROKEN DOWN INTO FATTY ACIDS.

WHAT IS A NUTRIENT?

Living things need nutrients to survive. We get many of our nutrients from food. There are lots of different types of nutrients that cells use to create energy. For example, some food is broken down into simple sugars. This isn't like the sugar in cakes and sweets – bread, rice, pasta and potatoes are all turned into simple sugars. Other foods that contain fat are broken down in to fatty acids. Fatty acids are used by the cells when simple sugars aren't available.

DISH OF THE DAY: ATP

Mitochondria create a chemical called ATP. ATP is the food that all cells use, and it is how they get their energy. There are a few ways that cells can make ATP, but mitochondria usually do it by putting a type of sugar called glucose with a type of gas called oxygen. When ATP breaks down, energy is created. The cell uses the energy to keep you alive and do all the things it needs to do.

SOME OF THE ENERGY CREATED WHEN MAKING ATP IS ALSO RELEASED AS HEAT TO KEEP YOUR BODY WARM.

Roll up, roll up, and take a look at one of the toughest organs out there. It's lean, it's mean, it's a cell-killing machine – it's the spleen! What do you mean you haven't heard of the spleen? Well, let's get learning.

STOP AT THE
SPLEEN

THE LIVER AND THE SPLEEN

The spleen is an organ with many jobs. One of these jobs is to take old, damaged cells from the blood. It does this by sorting through the cells as they go past – if the cells are healthy, they can carry on through the body. Any unhealthy cells are not allowed through. The liver is another very important organ that gets rid of old blood cells.

LIVER

SPLEEN

HOW ELSE ARE DAMAGED CELLS CLEANED UP?

There is a type of cell that eats up old and broken cells. These are called macrophages (say: mak-row-fay-jez). Macrophages exist all over the body, but many are found near the spleen and the liver. Macrophages gobble up damaged cells and break them apart. If they need to, they travel back to the liver and spleen, so the dead cells inside can be **recycled**.

MACROPHAGE

WHY DO CELLS DIE?

Sometimes cells are just not needed anymore. For example, some cells fight diseases. When the disease is gone, the cells have done their job, so they die. Cells also die to make up parts of the body. This is what happens on the top layer of your skin, which is completely made of dead cells. However, damaged or dying cells can be bad. If they break up in a dangerous way, the chemicals inside can spread to nearby, healthy cells and cause them damage.

Sometimes cells die because they get **infected** by diseases.

BAD CELL DEATHS CAN SOMETIMES LEAD TO DISEASES.

A GOOD DEATH

It is actually very important that cells die. Cells even have a special way of dying to make it safer for the body. The main way they do this is by taking themselves apart from the inside. The cell then breaks into small, safe packages that can be easily taken in by other cells. If a cell dies in this way, it is much easier for the body to clean up the mess left behind.

THIS CELL IS SAFELY DESTROYING ITSELF FROM WITHIN.

INTO THE
INTESTINES

WHAT ARE INTESTINES?

Your intestines are found inside your tummy. They are long tubes that snake from your stomach to your bum, carrying food. Muscles help the intestines squeeze the food through. As the food makes its way along the intestine, it is broken down, and nutrients and water are taken in by the body. The intestines are full of all sorts of important cells. There's only one problem. Most of them aren't human...

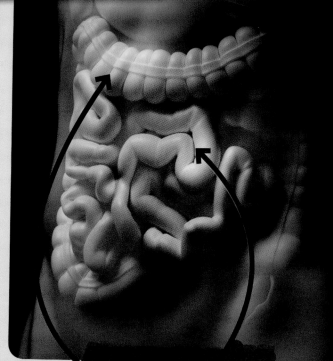

THE INTESTINES

MEET BACTERIA

Bacteria are living things that are made from only one cell. There are millions, maybe billions, of **species** of bacteria. They can be found everywhere in the world, from the tallest mountain to the bottom of the ocean. And they are also all over the outside and the inside of your body. Bacteria are different to animal and plant cells because they don't usually have organelles. All the different parts of a bacteria cell, including the DNA, are muddled up in the cytoplasm.

BACTERIA CELLS

THE MORE TYPES OF GOOD BACTERIA YOU HAVE IN YOUR INTESTINES, THE HEALTHIER YOU WILL BE.

Most of the time, bacteria are thought of as germs. It is true that many types of bad bacteria can make you very ill if they get into your body. They usually get in through your eyes, ears, mouth, or cuts in your skin. However, not all bacteria are bad. In fact, you wouldn't be able to survive without the ones in your intestines! They help your body break down your food.

HOW MANY BACTERIA CELLS LIVE INSIDE YOU?

There are trillions of bacteria cells inside of you. In fact, there are more bacteria cells in your body than human cells. Many of them are found in your intestines, but the biggest **diversity** of bacteria is on your forearm. It might not seem like it, but bacteria are everywhere, on every surface and object. It's just that they are too small to see without a microscope.

ALTHOUGH THE BACTERIA IN YOUR GUT IS GOOD, A LOT OF THE BACTERIA ON YOUR SKIN ISN'T. THIS IS WHY IT IS IMPORTANT TO WASH YOUR HANDS.

When bacteria break down your food, they release smelly gases and this is what causes you to... wait do you hear that rumbling? We'd better get out of here!

ENTER THE EYES

I've got some very interesting cells to show you next. Are you scared of people touching your eye? Well I hope our patient isn't, because we are going in!

I WANT TO KNOW WHAT LIGHT IS

When you look at an object, you are seeing the light bouncing off it and going into your eye. For example, the reason you can read these words is because light is hitting the page and bouncing in all sorts of directions. Some of this light gets into your eye.

LIGHT COMES FROM A LIGHT SOURCE, SUCH AS THE SUN OR AN ELECTRIC LIGHT.

PUPIL

IRIS

The pupil is the black part in the middle of your eye. It lets the light in. The iris is the colourful part around your pupil. It controls how big the pupil is, so more or less light passes through. The sclera is the white part. This is the outer layer of the eye.

SCLERA

THE MOST COMMON EYE COLOUR IS BROWN. BLUE, GREY, HAZEL AND GREEN ARE LESS COMMON. GREEN IS THE RAREST OF THESE COLOURS. WHAT IS YOUR EYE COLOUR?

THE FIRST HUMANS TO HAVE BLUE EYES APPEARED AROUND 10,000 YEARS AGO. HOWEVER, THE OLDEST POTTERY, WHICH WAS FOUND IN CHINA, IS AROUND 20,000 YEARS OLD. THAT MEANS THAT HUMANS HAVE HAD POTTERY LONGER THAN THEY'VE HAD BLUE EYES.

THE RETINA

The eye is a ball shape. The light passes through the pupil and lands on the back wall, which is called the retina. The retina is full of special cells which take in the light and send messages to the brain about what we are seeing. There are two types of these special cells: rods and cones.

RETINA

RODS

Rod cells can't see colour. Their job is to get a rough picture of what we are seeing. This means they look out for sizes, shapes and brightness. One human eye contains around 130 million rod cells. Rod cells are much more **sensitive** to light than cone cells.

ROD CELL

CONE CELL

CONES

There are a lot fewer cone cells than rod cells. A human eye contains around seven million cone cells. They are also shorter than rod cells. Cone cells are good at picking up the colour and **detail** of the outside world. Most cone cells are found in the middle of the retina.

FOLLOW THE
FAT CELLS

THE BODY'S CUSHION

Fat cells join together to create a type of fatty tissue. Fat is mainly found just underneath the skin and sometimes between muscles and organs. One of its main jobs is to act as a cushion to protect parts of the body.

THERE ARE TWO TYPES OF FAT CELL: BROWN AND WHITE. WHITE FAT CELLS CONTAIN MUCH BIGGER FAT DROPLETS INSIDE THAN BROWN ONES DO. BABIES HAVE A LOT OF BROWN FAT, WHILE ALMOST ALL FAT IN ADULTS IS WHITE.

FAT CELLS

JUST IN CASE

Fat is also something that the body uses for energy. It is stored in special fat cells. If your body needed energy, but there was none to use, it would take some of the fat around your body. Everyone needs a little bit of fat. However, too much fat can be unhealthy. Eating a healthy diet will give your body the perfect amount of fat.

A HEALTHY DIET CONTAINS LOTS OF VEGETABLES AND FRUIT.

BOING

BOING

Fat is soft and squishy. Not only does it help keep you warm and keep your organs safe, it also makes it much easier for little doctors like me to get around.

NERVE CELLS

Nerve cells send messages between the body and the brain or spinal cord. To do this, the nerve cells use electrical **signals**. There are lots of different signals that pass through nerve cells. For example, if you touch an object, nerves in your skin send messages to your brain telling you what that object feels like. When you want to move your fingers, a message is sent from your brain, through the nerves, to the muscles in your arm, telling it to move.

NERVE SIGNALS CAN TRAVEL VERY FAST, SOMETIMES AS FAST AS 431 KILOMETRES AN HOUR. THAT'S ALMOST FOUR TIMES AS FAST AS A CAR USUALLY TRAVELS!

NERVE CELL

NUCLEUS

AXON

DENTRITES

WHAT DO NERVE CELLS LOOK LIKE?

Nerve cells are long and thin. Like many other cells, they have a nucleus. Near the nucleus are the dendrites. Dendrites branch off from the cell and connect to other nerve cells. This allows messages to come in from other nerve cells around the body. The axon is the longest part of the nerve cell – it carries the message to the next nerve cell or body part. Axons are covered in a layer of fat to protect them.

THE LONGEST NERVE CELL IN YOUR BODY RUNS FROM YOUR SPINAL CORD TO YOUR TOES.

SEARCH FOR
SKIN CELLS

Your skin is the biggest organ in your body. It keeps all your insides on the inside, and the outside world on the outside. There are many layers to your skin. The top layer is the one you can see – this is also the layer that can feel. On the very top of this layer are the dead cells. Your skin is always shedding dead cells. The old cells are replaced by new ones rising from below.

LAYERS OF HUMAN SKIN

DIFFERENT CELLS

The most common cell in the top layer of your skin is filled with sacs of keratin. Keratin is the material that hair and nails are made from. Another type of cell found in the skin is called a melanocyte (say: mel-en-oh-site). One of the jobs of melanocytes is to protect the skin from the Sun. Although it is important to get some sunlight, too much can cause skin damage.

Melanocytes also produce a **pigment**. This can change the colour of someone's skin.

Where would we be without skin? All over the floor, probably.

MOVE TO THE
MUSCLE CELLS

Muscles move – that's what makes them special. Muscles help us run around, use our hands, and beat our siblings at sports, over and over again. We are going to talk about two types of muscles: skeletal and smooth.

SKELETAL MUSCLE UNDER A MICROSCOPE

SKELETAL MUSCLES

These are the muscles that help you walk around, jump up and down and make silly faces. They are attached to your skeleton with **tendons** so that they are able to move the bones. If you looked at a skeletal muscle under a microscope, it would look stripy. This is because it is full of long, stretchy cells. When your brain sends a signal to these skeletal muscles, the cells get shorter, and the muscle squeezes. This pulls on the tendons, and the bones and skin move.

SMOOTH MUSCLES

Many of your organs and insides are made up of smooth muscle. For example, the tube that connects your mouth to your stomach is covered in smooth muscle. This is so that food can be pushed along, like squeezing toothpaste out of a tube.

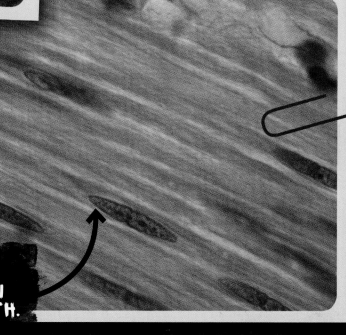

SMOOTH MUSCLE DOES NOT LOOK STRIPY UNDER A MICROSCOPE. AS YOU MIGHT HAVE GUESSED, IT LOOKS SMOOTH.

YOU CAN CONTROL YOUR SKELETAL MUSCLES, BUT YOUR SMOOTH MUSCLES MOVE AUTOMATICALLY.

BENEATH THE
BLOOD CELLS

RED BLOOD CELLS

If you've ever had a nose bleed, or if you have ever cut yourself, you already know a bit about red blood cells. Red blood cells are the main type of cell in our blood and they have a very important job: they carry oxygen from our lungs to all the cells that need it. The blood is pushed around the body through tubes called blood vessels. The heart is the pusher – it is beating all the time, so your blood never stops moving.

THERE ARE AROUND FOUR TO SIX LITRES OF BLOOD IN AN ADULT'S BODY.

RED BLOOD CELLS HAVE A SPECIAL SHAPE: THEY ARE CIRCLES WHICH ARE QUITE FLAT AND DIP IN THE MIDDLE.

Red blood cells live for around 120 days. They are different to other cells because they don't have as many organelles – for example, they get rid of their nucleus when they are still new and young. This is to make more room for oxygen.

RED BLOOD CELLS THAT ARE CARRYING OXYGEN MAKE THE BLOOD BRIGHT RED. IF THE BLOOD CONTAINS RED BLOOD CELLS THAT DON'T HAVE OXYGEN, IT IS MUCH DARKER.

The oxygen is connected to the red blood cell very tightly so it doesn't fall out! It might have to go a long way around the booddddyyyy!

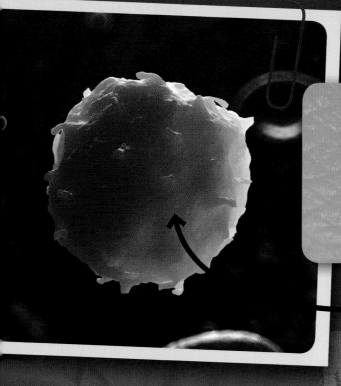

WHITE BLOOD CELLS

There are many different types of white blood cell, but they all have roughly the same job – to protect you from dangerous invaders. Things that cause illnesses, such as bacteria and viruses, get inside your body all the time. White blood cells are like bodyguards that show up to protect you.

WHITE BLOOD CELL

THE PERFECT TEAM

Some white blood cells raise the alarm if they find bad bacteria or viruses. The body can then send more white blood cells, which fight off invaders in different ways. Some cells gobble up and destroy bacteria. Other cells create things called antibodies. Antibodies are like little helpers which tag viruses and destroy them. Some white blood cells learn more about the bacteria or virus so that the body can be even better at fighting it next time.

ANTIBODIES

WELL, ALMOST THE PERFECT TEAM

Sometimes white blood cells can get it wrong, and attack things that aren't dangerous. This causes an allergy. People with allergies can get ill when they breathe in or eat things that aren't usually harmful. For example, some people are allergic to peanuts. Food allergies like this can be very serious. Some people have hay fever, which makes you sneeze, cough, and have a runny nose and eyes. This is caused by **pollen**. Hay fever is a less serious allergy, but it is still annoying.

29

ALL
BETTER

Oh no! Why, why, why is there a vacuum cleaner in here? And who left it on? It's been sucking up all the cells – no wonder the patient was ill!

Thank you so much for your help today. I couldn't have found the problem without you, my trusty assistant. Hopefully you learnt a few things about cells along the way.

So now you know all about the cells in the human body. Aren't they incredible? Here are some extra cell facts.

IF YOU UNRAVELED THE DNA INSIDE ONE OF YOUR CELLS, IT WOULD STRETCH OUT TO BECOME TWO METRES LONG. IF YOU STRETCHED OUT THE DNA FROM ALL YOUR CELLS AND PUT THEM END TO END, IT WOULD BE TWICE AS WIDE AS THE SOLAR SYSTEM.

AROUND FIVE MILLION CELLS ARE BUILT EVERY SECOND TO REPLACE DEAD CELLS.

IT TAKES ABOUT 60 SECONDS FOR CELLS TO TRAVEL AROUND THE BLOODSTREAM. AFTER TEN YEARS, THIS MEANS THE CELL COULD TRAVEL 96,000 KILOMETRES—IF THE CELL LIVED THAT LONG, OF COURSE.

GLOSSARY

AUTOMATICALLY	without conscious thought or control
BACTERIA	microscopic living things that can cause diseases
BALANCED DIET	eating a healthy selection of food each day, with lots of fruit and vegetables
BILLIONS	a billion is one thousand million
BLOODSTREAM	the flow of blood in living things
CHEMICALS	substances that materials are made from
DETAIL	small parts of something which can only be noticed when looked at carefully
DIVERSITY	a variety
GAS	an air-like substance that expands freely to fill any space available
INFECTED	contaminated with a virus and showing symptoms of illnesses
INSTRUMENT	an object that helps with a certain job
INTESTINES	long, coiled tubes below the stomach that help to digest food
MEMBRANE	a thin, soft, flexible layer
MUSCLE	bundles of tissue that can contract or squeeze together
NUTRIENTS	natural substances that plants and animals need to grow and stay healthy
ORGANS	(self-contained) parts of a living thing that have specific, important functions
PIGMENT	the natural colouring of a plant or animal
POLLEN	a powder-like substance made by plants
PREGNANT	when a mother develops a baby inside of her
RATE	how often something happens
RECYCLED	used again to make something else
SCAR TISSUE	a type of tissue that looks different, and is created to heal over deep cuts in the skin
SENSITIVE	good at sensing
SIGNALS	signs or actions which show information or instructions
SPECIES	a group of very similar animals or plants that are capable of producing young together
TENDONS	flexible cords that join muscles to bones
VIRUS	a microscopic thing which causes illness and disease in living things

INDEX